Called to Be a Catechist

The ROLE *of the*
CATECHIST

Inspiration and Professional Growth

TWENTY-THIRD
PUBLICATIONS
twentythirdpublications.com

IMPRIMATUR

+   Most Reverend
      Joseph R. Binzer
      Auxiliary Bishop
      Archdiocese of Cincinnati
      March 16, 2016

The *Imprimatur* ("Permission to
Publish") is a declaration that a book
or pamphlet is considered to be free
of doctrinal or moral error. It is not
implied that those who have granted
the *Imprimatur* agree with the contents,
opinions, or statements expressed.

Twenty-Third Publications
1 Montauk Avenue, Suite 200, New London, CT 06320
(860) 437-3012 » (800) 321-0411 » www.twentythirdpublications.com

ISBN: 978-1-62785-155-8
Library of Congress Catalog Card Number: 2015958562
Printed in the U.S.A.

CONTENTS

INTRODUCTION

One of the first questions any new catechist asks is, "What's my role?" In 2005 the United States Conference of Catholic Bishops published the *National Directory for Catechesis* (NDC) to help answer that question. This document offers catechists a compass to encourage, support, and enhance the meaning, direction, and impact of the Church's catechetical ministry.

Our vocation as catechists is to deepen our personal relationship with Jesus Christ by growing in holiness and knowledge of our faith. Accepting our catechetical vocation is an intentional act or confirmation that we are willing to stay the course and to open ourselves to God's self-communication. The NDC states: "The object of catechesis is communion with Jesus Christ. Catechesis leads people to enter the mystery of Christ, to encounter him, and to discover themselves and the meaning of their lives in him" (n. 19 B).

Our vocation as catechists is a "pivotal dimension of the Church's pastoral activity and a significant element in all the Church does to hand on the faith" (NDC, n. 19C). This is an awesome responsibility and a task in which we are privileged to participate. Thus it is imperative that we prayerfully reflect on the vision the bishops have set for us.

To further aid in defining the role of the catechist, the NDC outlines six important tasks. The catechist is invited to participate in each of these tasks. So, in this book about the catechist's role, the chapters highlight those tasks. You are encouraged to read, reflect on, and dialogue with other catechists about the insights you gain from your reading.

This book is written by leaders/practitioners who are or have been engaged in the formation of catechists. Because they have spent quality time studying the direction, meaning, and impact of the NDC, you can enrich your experience by holding the NDC in one hand and this book in the other to discern how to become more effective as a catechist.

CATECHESIS: SOURCES, NATURE, *and* PURPOSE

SUE GRENOUGH

Christ
yesterday and today;
the Beginning and the End;
the Alpha; and the Omega.
All time belongs to him;
and all the ages.
To him be glory and power;
through every age
and forever.

The priest proclaims these words as he carves the alpha, the omega, and the year on the new paschal candle at the Easter Vigil. This proclamation defines the heart of our faith, the person of Jesus Christ, the Word of God. Christ is the Alpha and Omega, the beginning and the end of all that exists. Sacred Scripture and the documents of the Church affirm the centrality of Jesus Christ. He is source and center of a catechist's faith. He is the heart of all catechetical efforts.

There are two dimensions of a catechist: development as a person and growth as a minister. On a personal level, catechists can be assured of help in developing their own spirituality and in living as disciples of Christ. For the ministry, catechists can anticipate formation in the knowledge and skills of transmitting the Good News of Jesus Christ.

Wise Guidance

At the direction of the Second Vatican Council, universal and national directories have been published and revised to give vision and direction to catechetical ministry in the universal and national churches.

The revised *National Directory for Catechesis* (NDC) outlines the source and goal of all catechesis in the United States. "The definitive aim of catechesis is to put people not only in touch but in communion, in intimacy, with Jesus Christ: only he can lead us to the love of the Father in the Spirit and make us share in the life of the Holy Trinity" (NDC, n. 19B).

"In touch," "in communion," "in intimacy with Jesus Christ": these powerful words provide a glimpse into the lifelong journey for all Christians—to know and recognize Jesus Christ. As the relationship with Christ unfolds, the believer seeks to follow him more closely by becoming his disciple. The life of the disciple proclaims Jesus Christ in all aspects of life, as Christ is proclaimed at the Easter Vigil every year.

To develop and nourish this relationship with Jesus is a theme firmly rooted in the experiences of the covenants of the Old and New Testaments. Gradually, God sought over and over again a deepening relationship with the Jewish people through various covenants, especially the one at Mt. Sinai through Moses (see Exodus 19).

In all these covenants, God assures the people that he will be their God and they are his chosen ones. The covenants of the Old Testament found fulfillment in the new covenant of Jesus, where divinity and humanity were perfectly expressed: "He is the new and eternal covenant whose blood 'will be shed on behalf of many for the forgiveness of sins' so that humanity may be redeemed and restored to communion with God" (NDC, n. 34).

So this is the vision! The task and work of catechesis is to align the practices of catechesis with this vision. Yet, in the midst of schedules, lesson plans, notes to parents, etc., is this goal of catechesis obvious? How does a catechist grow personally in the knowledge of Christ to the point of communion and intimacy? What are those efforts that best make Christ visible, known, and followed? What are those efforts that make this conversion, this turning to Christ as the center of life, into a living, explicit, and fruitful confession of faith?

Growing in Faith and Discipleship

This task of putting the vision into practice could seem overwhelming if it were not for all the supports at the disposal of the catechist. For the personal faith life of the catechist, the community of believers provides prayer and liturgy, witness as disciples, insights of theology, and moral values evident in Church and society.

In the liturgy, Christ is present and experienced in word, in community, in the Body of Christ, and in the priest. By immersing oneself in this mystery regularly, the catechist receives the nourishment to know Christ more fully and to find ways to live as his disciple. Also, the community, through its witness of living the word of God, gives strength to one another as they strive to know Christ in ever new ways. Many parish communities are composed of smaller communities organized around prayer and study, peer ministry, or life issues. These groups strive to make more evident the connection between faith and life.

> Through their own life of witness, catechists become the "echo of the Good News," which the word "catechesis" originally signifies in Greek.

The catechist also has rich resources in Scripture and prayer. Prayer "expresses the covenant relationship that binds God to the person and the person to God" (NDC, n. 34). Various prayer forms combine prayer with Scripture. Many communities are praying together using *lectio divina*, which is a meditative form of reading and listening to Scripture. The tradition of the Catholic Church has a treasury of prayer forms which can nurture the faith at any stage of life.

Through their own personal witness, catechists give meaning and expression to the message they communicate. Through their own life of witness, catechists become the "echo of the Good News," which the word "catechesis" originally signifies in Greek.

Growing in Knowledge and Skill

In the exercise of their ministry, catechists simultaneously grow as they call other believers to grow in faith. While catechists grow in knowledge of their faith in their personal faith experience, they also seek the knowledge that is specific to their area of catechesis.

If a catechist is serving in the catechumenate, for example, the focus will be the basics of the Catholic faith, the elements of the initiation process, the learning styles of the learners, and even knowledge about the faith traditions of the candidates and catechumens. Catechists preparing believers for the first reception of Eucharist will steep themselves in the mystery of Eucharist.

Communicating the Faith

Catechesis is about communication of the faith in Jesus Christ, either as beginning faith or deepening faith. Catechists, then, need to become skilled in divine and human methodology, in constructing learning experiences appropriate to the age of the learners, in assessing individual learning styles, in catechetical process, and in blending all of this to achieve the goal of faith in a Person.

With the assurance of the call to ministry, the catechist has rich traditions and resources in the Church, and particularly from within their contemporary faith community, from which to draw.

There is a difference between an information-centered program and a discipleship-centered program. Perhaps a blend of the two is possible where discipleship, a way of life, is learned and practiced with supportive learning. While discipleship includes affective learning, one needs the informed wisdom of the past and present Church for living authentic faith. Periodic reviews of catechetical efforts are in order to assure that the desired result is, in fact, the actual result.

Conclusion

At the beginning of this chapter we remembered the Easter proclamation of Jesus Christ, the beginning and end for all ages. Jesus Christ, as the Word of God, is the source for all catechesis. This Word of God is celebrated in the community of believers in prayer, service, and the personal and communal lives of the members. Developing a relationship with Jesus Christ throughout one's life is the object of all catechesis.

For catechists, this vision provides both direction and challenge for their ministry. Catechists focus their efforts on providing the means to nurture a relationship with Jesus Christ and live as his disciple. Catechetical plans and activities are chosen and evaluated in terms of this goal.

To do this, catechists use the knowledge and skills they acquire as ministers of the Word of God as well as the grace that accompanies their vocation. Then they can truly say with Paul, "For to me, life is Christ" (Philippians 1:21).

Your Thoughts

1 What steps have I taken to nurture or deepen my relationship with Jesus? (Be specific.)

_____

_____

_____

_____

2 What "covenant" biblical narratives can I recall? What meaning do they have for my spiritual life?

_____

_____

_____

_____

Try This

Fold an 8½" X 11" sheet of paper in thirds. Position the paper horizontally so that the folds indicate columns. In the first column, list all the resources you have to support your catechetical ministry. In the second (middle) column, list the resources you need but do not have (your dream list). In the third column, design a plan of action to acquire these resources.

PROMOTING KNOWLEDGE *of the* FAITH

ROSE L. BENNETT

When Catholics profess the Creed during Mass, we proclaim the core beliefs that form the context of our actions, decisions, and attitudes: We believe in one God: God the Father, God the Son incarnate in Jesus Christ, and God the Holy Spirit, who enlightens, guides, strengthens, and consoles us.

For some of us, these beliefs were part of our Catholic upbringing; others of us came to faith as adults through the witness of believers. Our faith, too, is influenced by life events, and shapes the directions of our lives.

Our Creed is brief, but the truths it contains warrant a lifetime of reflection and study so that the "We believe" of the gathered community is an "I believe" for each disciple.

Catechists as Witnesses of Faith

The role of catechists is to guide children, youth, and adults on their journeys of faith. We consider our call a privilege and an obligation that flows from our baptismal mission to continue the work of Jesus Christ.

It is only in witnessing to our own faith and beliefs that we can be effective evangelizing catechists. The first step in living out our call to catechesis is to reflect on the beliefs that have shaped our lives and our knowledge of the faith we profess. When we witness to Jesus from the depths of our own experience, we not only engage in evangelizing catechesis, we also find that our own faith grows stronger.

> How does our faith provide answers to the complexity of life?
>
> Is the gospel still relevant?

The United States bishops' pastoral plan for adult faith formation, *Our Hearts Were Burning Within Us,* reiterates from the *General Directory for Catechesis* that mature faith is living, explicit, and fruitful (see GDC, n. 82). Passing on the teachings of our Church as found in the Creed provides for the continuing development of a mature faith. The doctrine that we learned as children in a simple form we examine anew as we progress through the stages of adulthood.

Technological and scientific advances of the twenty-first century challenge the surety of our childhood faith. We grapple with issues such as stem cell research, end-of-life decisions, consumerism, divorce and remarriage, and many more. Will our faith sustain us when faced with such challenges? How does our faith provide answers to the complexity of life? Is the gospel still relevant?

The "stuff" of the front page of our newspapers and advice columns mirrors today's concerns. By bringing these issues into dialogue with Catholic doctrine, catechists motivate people to delve more deeply into the truths we profess. After all, we know that we learn best when we have a question that needs an answer, when we have a problem to solve, and when we face a difficult decision.

By looking at the concerns and needs of the different populations within our parish, we can plan our catechesis so that it responds to the questions with which people are grappling.

Beliefs Express Faith

The human spirit yearns to make sense of life. Peoples of all times and cultures have intuited the divine and attempted to articulate what they know in the depths of their being. "Who is God? How does God act in the world? What is God's relationship with humanity?"

In striving to express and communicate their faith, people have used art, music, poetry, and story. Intellectual expressions of faith are called *beliefs*. The *Catechism of the Catholic Church* states, "Communion in faith needs a common language of faith, normative for all and uniting all in the same confession of faith" (CCC, n. 185).

Thus, in the early centuries of Christianity, Christians gathered their beliefs into professions of faith or creedal statements. They are called professions of faith because "they summarize the faith that Christians profess. They are called 'creeds' on account of what is usually their first word in Latin: *credo* ('I believe')" (CCC, n. 187).

While there have been many creeds formulated throughout the history of the Church, they have all expressed the one faith, "received from the one Lord, transmitted by one Baptism, and grounded in the conviction that all people have only one God and Father" (CCC, n. 172).

The Apostles' Creed dates back to Rome in the centuries following the time of Christ. It was a summary of Christian doctrine for those preparing to enter the Church through baptism. The Nicene Creed resulted from the first two ecumenical councils of 325 (Nicea) and 381 (Constantinople), which sought to clarify the relationship between the Father and Son and between the Spirit and Father and Son. In 2011, a few revisions returned the wording of the Creed to the more literal English translation of the Latin.

As catechists, it is our task to hand on what we believe and pray—to lead others to the confession of faith in God—Father, Son, and Holy Spirit.

We Believe in God...Creator of Heaven and Earth

We know God as creator, and we share in God's creative activity when we care for the environment—plant flowers, paint a picture, compose a poem, or teach a child to read. When faced with the beauty that surrounds us in nature and in the faces of our brothers and sisters, how can we help but be people with grateful hearts?

In Jesus, God became man so that we can better know him. We can know God as loving, forgiving, and healing. Through study of the gospels we come to know more clearly the God who loved us into being; who became incarnate in Jesus to show us the way to walk, the truth to tell, and the life to live; and who is with us always through the Holy Spirit.

> A central doctrine of Christianity is that God loves every human being. Therefore, we are required to do so as well.

As God is revealed in relationship of Father, Son, and Spirit, God calls us into relationship not only with God but with all peoples as sons and daughters of God, made in the divine image. A central doctrine of Christianity is that God loves every human being. We are called to share in that love and to love others as God has loved us.

Communities debate issues of migrant workers, racial profiling, affordable housing, and minimum wage. Christians themselves are divided into camps of varying degrees of "orthodoxy" over issues concerning human sexuality, right to life, and the death penalty. Yet, even as we claim relationship with brothers and sisters in Christ, opinions, misconceptions, and lack of clear understanding of Church teaching alienate us from one another.

Catechesis provides opportunities for engaging in discussion and dialogue where learners express ideas, listen to the opinions of others, and evaluate differing views—with the Church's teaching as a consistent compass.

We Believe in Jesus Christ, our Lord

Catechists keep in mind that "Jesus Christ not only transmits the Word of God: he *is* the Word of God" (*General Directory for Catechesis or* GDC,

n. 98). Our teaching, therefore, must engage not only the mind but also the heart, and it must transform the behavior of our learners. Ours is not to be a private faith but a faith lived out in community.

Mother Teresa often spoke of the hungry in our midst—those not hungry for bread but for a smile, an understanding word, a kind touch. She admonished us to be aware of the lonely ones right in our own families. Jesus reminds us of the sacredness of shared meals. He ate dinner with sinners, provided a picnic lunch for thousands who came to hear him speak, and fixed breakfast for his disciples.

Mary, the mother of Jesus, is not only a model of holiness but also a model of service. Her concern for her cousin Elizabeth and for the bride and groom at Cana, her presence at the foot of the cross, her courage as the body of Jesus was placed in her arms: this is the empathetic love to which we too are called. Catechists teach most profoundly when we are truly present to one another and put aside our own concerns to listen well to the children and adults we encounter in our ministry.

Because of the resurrection of Jesus Christ, we believe that God can use our suffering to bring us blessings and deeper faith. Jesus' passion and death on a cross was not the end but the beginning of new life. We name this the paschal mystery, and we share in its promise. Our faith and a supportive community bring light out of the darkness of loss and death. As we provide opportunities for learners to reflect upon and share their stories, they come to see how often it is the darkness itself that helps us to see the light more clearly.

Our belief in the communion of saints speaks of our assurance that physical death opens up to a glorified eternal life. We are one with our loved ones who have gone before us. As we remember and celebrate those whose lives have shaped ours, they are truly alive in our hearts. Their presence is real to us as we find ourselves quoting their words, remembering their guidance and advice, laughing at happy memories, and telling their stories.

Ah, the stories! The Church celebrates the life-giving stories of those we honor as canonized saints. The lessons of humility and love and service and courage taught to us by the saints resonate across the centuries. We share these stories with those we teach to gift them with examples of faith and to provide them with spiritual friends for life.

I Believe in the Holy Spirit

The Holy Spirit was present at the first moment of creation. In Genesis 1, God created "the heavens and the earth" out of nothing. God breathed the breath of life into the first person (see Genesis 2:7). Isaiah exalted that "the spirit of the Lord GOD is upon me" (Isaiah 61:1).

In the story of the Annunciation in Luke's gospel, the angel tells Mary, "The Holy Spirit will come upon you and the power of the Most High will overshadow you" (Luke 1:35). Jesus promised that he would not leave us orphans but would send the Holy Spirit to be with us always to guide us and remind us of all that Jesus taught (John 14:26). On the first Easter evening, the resurrected Jesus breathed on his gathered Apostles and said, "Receive the holy Spirit" (John 20:22). And on Pentecost, the Spirit came upon those gathered, drove out their fear, and filled them with such zeal that they willingly went forth to preach the gospel of Jesus (Acts 2:4).

The good news is that this same Spirit is with each of us today. God entrusts us with bringing forth the reign of God. To accomplish this, we believe that God gives each of us unique gifts and talents in order to bring light to the world.

As we reflect on the problems and crises that face the global community today, it is easy to become numb and to despair of being able to effect any change for the better. Yet when we name the Holy Spirit as Lord and Giver of Life, we claim the life-giving power that enables us to be agents of change. We believe that the Holy Spirit guides the Church in her mission of embracing the whole world and calling the world to holiness.

Conclusion

To a violent culture, catechists bring the message of peace. Where death dominates the news, we preach the dignity of life. When revenge masquerades as justice, we speak of forgiveness. As the craving for more and more material goods threatens the very existence of our earth, we teach concern and care for all of creation.

"The catechist is essentially a mediator [who facilitates] communication between the people and the mystery of God, between subjects amongst themselves, as well as with the community" (GDC, n. 156). The truths of our Tradition are vibrant messages that bring hope and meaning to life. Catechists help others grow in their understanding and knowledge of Catholic teaching so that all can confidently proclaim, "This is our faith. This is the faith of the Church. We are proud to profess it, in Christ Jesus our Lord!"

Your Thoughts

1 Reflecting on my own faith journey, the following persons have been most significant in forming me as a Catholic Christian. After each name, I list the way the person is or was significant in that role.

_____

_____

_____

2 How has my image of God changed from when I was young? To which Person of the Trinity do I find myself praying most often?

_____

_____

_____

Try This

Slowly recite the Apostles' or Nicene Creed. Consider the words carefully. Which phrases speak to your heart? Which are most clear to you? Are there any articles of the Creed whose meanings are obscure to you?

LITURGY *and* SACRAMENTS

JOYCE ANN ZIMMERMAN, C.PP.S.

L iturgy is officially defined as the celebration of the seven sacraments and the Liturgy of the Hours.

For the majority of us, however, our most frequent liturgical experience is the Eucharistic celebration of Sunday Mass. Full, conscious, and active participation is essential; we can't come to liturgy and be bumps on a log. Nevertheless, what is really happening at liturgy is what God is doing within us; all we need do is surrender ourselves to this divine action and be transformed into more perfect members of the body of Christ.

Celebrating Well

In order for our surrender and God's fruitful action to happen, catechesis on liturgy must

> The first task of liturgical catechesis... is to help our young members...to surrender to God's action, encounter God during the liturgy, and be transformed to live more perfectly as followers of Christ.

be more than simply teaching information about the different liturgies and what is happening—the meaning of the different symbols, gestures, postures, words, and actions and how God works through them. At some point, of course, these things must be taught. But sometimes we can get so caught up in information that we forget what is most important about catechesis.

The word *catechesis* comes from two Greek words: *kata* (down) and *echein* (to sound). Therefore, literally, *katechein* (catechesis) means to "sound down." This is the basic notion of Tradition: we hand down the truths of our faith to those who come after us.

Handing down the doctrines of our faith is very important indeed. But when it comes to liturgical catechesis, the better place to begin is with celebrating well the liturgy itself.

The first task of liturgical catechesis, then, is to help our young members of the Catholic community to *surrender* to God's action, *encounter* God during the liturgy, and *be transformed* to live more perfectly as followers of Christ. This experience cannot be taught in a classroom; it is something parents and catechists witness to and model. It is less teaching and more *proclaiming*.

Preparation for proclaiming the word means more than checking word pronunciation. What is proclaimed is the conviction of the lector's lived experience of the Scripture selection. *Living* the word is what really is proclaimed to the liturgical assembly.

Liturgy and the Paschal Mystery

When we think of the term *paschal mystery,* we sometimes limit our thoughts to Jesus' death and resurrection. Saint Paul in his letter to the Philippians takes in the whole mystery, starting with the Incarnation: "Have in you the same attitude that is also yours in Christ Jesus. Who, though he was in the form of God, did not regard equality with God something to be grasped. Rather he emptied himself, taking the form of a slave, coming in human likeness, and found human in appearance, he humbled himself becoming obedient to death, even death on a cross"

(Philippians 2:5–8). We ought also to consider Jesus' public ministry and how he had always done "just as the Father has commanded" (John 14:31).

The key to understanding the paschal mystery, then, is to remember that Jesus did his Father's will. He was the obedient Son from the very first breath of his human life. Jesus' life is a model of obedience and self-giving and how these lead to new, risen life. Through word and sacrament we encounter the obedient and self-giving Christ Jesus.

At the Last Supper, when Jesus commanded his disciples to "do this in memory of me" (Luke 22:19), he was telling us more than that we must simply go to Mass. He was telling us that every time we celebrate liturgy we "do this"—we make present Jesus' dying and rising, his obedience and self-giving, so that we might be transformed and become more perfectly obedient and self-giving and thus, with him, rise to new life.

The tremendous gift of liturgy is that the risen Christ is present to us not as a far-off God but as a lover who embraced all our humanity except sin so that we might share in his divine life. The paschal mystery, then, is not so much a concept to be understood, as it is a *person*, Jesus Christ, obedient and self-giving.

> The tremendous gift of liturgy is that the risen Christ is present to us not as a far-off God but as a lover who embraced all our humanity except sin so that we might share in his divine life.

Jesus' mystery becomes our own mystery at our baptism. St. Paul asks, "Are you unaware that we who were baptized into Christ Jesus were baptized into his death?…So that…we too might live in newness of life" (Romans 6:3–4).

Unfortunately, Paul's question seems to pass us by at times. We sometimes forget how important baptism is. More than a ritual which happened to most of us when we were infants, baptism is an ongoing, daily commitment to live the paschal mystery. Each time we say yes to dying to ourselves, to self-giving for the sake of others, we ratify again and again our baptismal promises—to live like Christ, to take up our own cross daily, to be as caring and loving as Jesus.

The paschal mystery—suffering and joy, dying and rising—is not a matter of "paying our dues" so that we might be "rewarded." Rather, Jesus taught that we must take up our own cross and lose our lives for the sake of others (see Matthew 16:24–25). In this very self-giving, God raises us to new life. Thus, in the dying is the rising. How breathtaking is this heart of liturgy!

The Liturgical Assembly: Body of Christ Made Visible

In liturgy we make present and celebrate (enact) the paschal mystery, the dying and rising of Jesus. Yet the paschal mystery implies two other Christian realities.

First, we are never alone in celebrating or living this mystery. We are the body of Christ, a community joined with one another by sharing a common identity. Second, the paschal mystery is how we must live every day. The dying and rising defines our everyday Christian living. We now consider these two aspects of paschal mystery in more detail.

In a society that hallows rugged individualism, in which families are scattered and neighbors are strangers, in which loneliness and home-lessness are pandemic, and in which parishes are clustered or becoming mega-churches, it is sometimes hard to imagine how we can have any sense of being a Christian community.

Who are we when we worship? Certainly, we are not simply a gaggle of individuals. One effect of baptism that deserves much more reflection is that when we are plunged into the dying and rising mystery of Christ in baptism (see, for example, Romans 6:3–11), we are given a unique share in divine life. The Holy Spirit comes to dwell within us and we are changed forever! We receive a new identity as daughters and sons of God; we become members of the body of Christ.

Practically speaking, this means that every baptized member of the Church shares exactly the same identity; we are "grafted" onto the risen

Christ and share his new life (see John 15:1–17). Each of us, by our baptism, is the presence of the risen Christ for all those we meet!

The amazing thing that happens as we gather for liturgy is that, in crossing the portal of the church, we surrender our individual selves into God's hands in order to become bigger than we are. We unite ourselves with Christ, the head of the body made visible in the person of the ordained priest, and in this act of self-surrender, the body of Christ is one. The Church is made visible.

This is why surrendering ourselves to the liturgical action, placing ourselves on the altar with the bread and wine so that we too are transformed more perfectly into being the body of Christ, is so important to the whole liturgical action. This is our entry into the dying and rising mystery.

Liturgy is always the *communal* act of the whole body of Christ united with its head. Liking the songs, the homily, or how the liturgy flows—as important as these are—is less important than each of us surrendering ourselves into God's hands so that God can transform us. This isn't something that is always noticeable; we won't always be hit over the head with divine presence at liturgy. But gradually, over time, God shapes us into more perfect images of the divine Son.

It is this *encounter* between the divine and the human taking place in liturgy which is transforming and life-giving. This is how we are sent forth: not just with the good feelings of having given an hour or so to God in worship, but with the challenge to be Christ's risen presence for all those we meet.

Liturgy Challenges Us To Be the Presence of the Risen Christ in Our Daily Living

Understanding the relationship of liturgy and life hinges on appreciating our identity as the body of Christ: by being grafted onto Christ in baptism we take up his saving mission. Liturgy is not simply for us; it is for the sake of others as well. Our participation in liturgy makes demands on us; our daily living can never be the same.

Imagine what our families, parishes, classrooms, communities, country, and world would be like if we *really* functioned out of a profound awareness of ourselves and others as members of the body of Christ!

Would generosity of spirit be so difficult if we truly realized that building up another is building up ourselves (since we share a common identity)? Would we be so quick to judge, condemn, slander, take advantage of, and criticize others if we realized that tearing down others harms ourselves as well?

> Because of our unity in the one body of Christ, no act—no matter how seemingly small and insignificant—is unimportant.

It may sound preposterous to assert that *we* can change the world. Most of us are not called to perform world-shattering, heroic actions (although being a catechist always has its moments which call for heroism). Liturgy, however, helps us realize our shared identity, our solidarity with one another in the one body of Christ. Liturgy helps us remember that the world is changed when we ourselves do the little, everyday things as Christ would. We do this because we remember that we ourselves are the presence of the risen Christ in our fractured world.

Realizing our identity helps us to act consistently as Christ's risen presence. As we change our behaviors, and ourselves, the goodness ripples out. The world *is* changed, because affecting one member of the body affects all members. Because of our unity in the one body of Christ, no act—no matter how *seemingly* small and insignificant—is unimportant. And every act is a kind of liturgy offering God praise and thanksgiving.

For example, patiently smiling at the rambunctious student is daily liturgy; giving extra time to the troubled youngster is daily liturgy; welcoming and encouraging all these precious ones of God is daily liturgy; modeling goodness and God's graciousness for them is daily liturgy.

This ought to give us courage. Christ does not ask us to become someone we are not. Rather, he asks us to do our daily tasks with our

Christian identity in mind. Liturgy (and especially the Eucharist) reminds us—and teaches us—that who we are is the body of Christ sent on mission to bring salvation to all, thus continuing Jesus' own ministry.

We are not called simply to be catechists *teaching* our faith; we are called to be witnesses of the loving presence of Christ, to do *everything* as if it were Christ himself acting. No matter where we are or what we are doing, we are asked to surrender ourselves for the good of others.

This may seem like a daunting task—to be the body of Christ, self-sacrificing for the sake of others. We sometimes forget that being the presence of the risen Christ for others is not something that unfolds in big, showy ways. It unfolds in the simple things of our ordinary days.

This is the most important task of the catechist. By modeling genuine love and respect for the youngsters as members of the body of Christ, we instill in them a sense of their own goodness as daughters and sons of God. When catechists teach out of a genuine awe for the mystery we are privileged to live, students begin to catch this as what is most important about the catechetical process. These are not simply classes during which we teach about our faith; the classes themselves are a kind of liturgy during which Christ is encountered and catechist and students alike are transformed.

Conclusion

Take time during each catechetical class or session simply to be still, to open the space to encounter God, and to teach youngsters that in the stillness God comes to teach, guide, strengthen, and transform them. When we model and teach youngsters the quietness and gentleness of life, we give them life lessons that accompany them on their whole life's journey, a Christian journey that leads them to their ultimate identity and destiny—fullness of life with God forever.

Your Thoughts

1 What new ideas for catechizing have I found in this chapter?

_____

_____

2 How can I implement these in my catechesis?

_____

_____

Try This

Make a chart of two columns, one column labeled "Self-giving, Dying to Self" and the other labeled "Joy of New Life." As you live your week, think of the times you died to self, and reflect on the good that came out of that; note these thoughts on the chart.

Also think of the joys you've experienced and note what dying by you or someone else had to take place so that you could have that joy; note these thoughts as well.

This exercise helps you become more aware of the times you actually lived the dying and rising mystery of Christ.

Moral Formation *in* Christ

PATRICK R. GUENTERT

I n contemporary society there are many challenges to the dignity of the human person. The *National Directory of Catechesis* states, "at the center of the moral vision contained in this nation's founding documents are two basic principles: (1) the recognition of the dignity and rights of the human person as endowed by their Creator and (2) liberty and justice for all" (n. 41B).

Most of us are aware of the areas where these principles are under siege today. They include abortion, euthanasia, biological and technological advances, and the treatment of immigrants and undocumented immigrants. In his 1995 encyclical titled *The Gospel of Life*, Pope John Paul II gathered these under the title of "culture of death." The poison of this culture seems to be spreading across the whole earth in our day. It seems that no human life is safe or dignified.

The NDC goes on to say that in the United States we live "in a society that publicly proclaims that liberty is an inalienable right," but "freedom has come to mean an unlimited individual autonomy in which many people find their ultimate sense of fulfillment in the exercise of unrestricted personal choice. Individual freedom becomes the absolute and the source of other values" (n. 42B). Excessive individualism runs counter to the teachings of Jesus, and the formation of faith communities that support us in our struggle to live a good life.

Catechesis on Christian Morality
In this light, the NDC (n. 41B), urges us to offer a catechesis on Christian morality that

- Upholds the right to life from conception to natural death;

- Presents the distinctively Christian understanding of human freedom;

- Teaches that freedom reaches its authentic goal in love of the weak and defenseless and in defense of their rights;

- Promotes the public expression of the Christian faith in the formation of social policy;

- Encourages concern for the lives of the poor, the weak, the disabled, and the sick, as well as action on their behalf;

- Helps the faithful to make practical moral decisions in the light of the gospels;

- Encourages the faithful to understand that power, wealth, utility, and productivity must be subordinated to and guided by higher moral value.

If we apply the above principles regarding the dignity of the human person, where does the pattern for our moral living come from?

If morality is the way we live because of our awareness of the presence of God, Christian morality is the way we live because of the passion, death, and resurrection of Jesus Christ and our awareness that Jesus did this for us both personally and as Church.

The distinction between the two was laid out in the *General Directory for Catechesis* (GDC): "The Sermon on the Mount, in which Jesus takes up the Decalogue, and impresses upon it the spirit of the beatitudes, is an indispensable point of reference for the moral formation which is most necessary today" (n. 85).

Briefly, what this means from a scriptural standpoint is that in the Old Testament, God calls Moses to the top of Mount Sinai, where he receives the Ten Commandments. In the context of the scriptural story, God fulfills the promise to Abraham to create a people by presenting a band of rag-tag ex-slaves with ten preventative measures to help them form the nation of Hebrew people.

In Matthew's gospel, Jesus parallels this by going up on a mountain, seating himself, and proclaiming the Beatitudes. These are positive goals toward which his followers are to strive. Between the Old and the New Testament, we have the framework for our moral life: the Ten Commandments, below which we dare not sink lest we jeopardize our ability to form community; and the Beatitudes, which are the goal toward which we strive in order to follow Christ, who is the norm of our moral life.

How can we live out the Beatitudes? Not on our own. We need God's grace. Sanctifying grace is God's life within us, given through God's free initiative—not because we did anything to earn it. Our moral life is grounded in the three theological virtues of Faith, Hope, and Charity.

Such grace transforms human nature. In addition, God also gives daily actual grace to help us develop those good habits of behavior we call moral virtues, represented by the cardinal, or hinge, virtues of Prudence, Justice, Fortitude, and Temperance. Parents and catechists need to recognize, praise, and encourage behaviors that help in the formation of virtues.

A Formed and Informed Conscience

The *Catechism of the Catholic Church* defines conscience as "a judgment of reason whereby the human person recognizes the moral quality of a concrete act" (n. 1778). Each person is born with the ability to make such judgments, but it takes time to develop a well-formed conscience.

From the beginning of life, the formation of conscience is aided by the good influence of others. Loving parents give an infant the beginning of a sense of dignity by the way they instruct their child in proper behavior. Good parenting gives the child both a healthy sense of self-worth and the recognition of being loved, which provide a solid foundation for the formation of a good conscience.

Nevertheless, not all input from parents, conscious or unconscious, is helpful. For example, a small child is taught not to break things around the house. But accidents happen, and the child bursts into tears because he or she broke a window or a lamp. It is important in parenting as well as in catechizing to note the difference between the feelings of guilt that come from accidents or mistakes and the moral guilt that comes from choosing to do what is wrong. It takes some time for any person to learn the difference between accidents and intentions.

How parents and other adults react and how they treat the child will have a lot to do with the child learning to understand moral responsibility. Parents and catechists can assist the child in realizing that regular prayer, careful and wise instruction, and learning and understanding the teachings of the Church are helps to making good moral choices throughout one's whole life.

Approaching the Church's Teaching on Morality

The Church is a community in which the demands of God are kept alive by speaking about them so they are never forgotten, and, more importantly, by continuing to ask what those demands mean right here and right now.

All of us who compose the Church—pope, bishops, priests, and baptized laity—bear a responsibility to be faithful to God's commandments and to live good moral lives. As a safeguard, Jesus Christ has given to his Church—Saint Peter and his successors—Teaching Authority. The

Magisterium of the Church, including the teachings of the popes and councils, provides one of the most important tools for the formation of conscience and living a moral life.

Although all the members of the Church seek to understand how to obey the commandments and live a moral life in accord with the gospel, the Holy Father and the bishops in union with him bear a special responsibility in assisting in moral formation. Each member of the Church, when trying to be assured that his or her judgment about the rightness or wrongness of a thought or an action is correct, must take the teaching of the Church with utmost seriousness, for that teaching expresses the belief of the whole community concerning God's will.

Nevertheless, the individual is not exempted from making a personal decision. Each person has to make that "reasoned judgment" as to the rightness or wrongness of an action. Through prayer and reflection, we come into contact with God, who reveals the kind of person he wants us to become. We have to decide whether certain actions or attitudes will help us or hinder us from becoming that person.

The formation of conscience is, in reality, a lifelong task. We do not wake up one day with a fully formed conscience. That is why the practice of virtue is so very important. That practice helps us habitually to act in accord with the gospel and the teaching of the Church. It is a most important catechetical task to assist those we teach both in gaining sufficient knowledge and in understanding the consequences of their actions so that good habits can be cultivated.

Crucial to conscience formation and following the teaching of the Church is our relationship with Christ nourished through prayer, study, and the frequent reception of the sacraments—especially Eucharist and reconciliation. As our relationship with Christ grows, we will also grow

> Through prayer and reflection, we come into contact with God, who reveals the kind of person God wants us to become.

in our understanding of Church teaching and the requirements of our life in Christ.

The Meaning of Sin

Sin is rejecting God's love, God's plan for us. Sin is both an action and the result of what our life has become. It is the exact opposite of virtue. Where virtue is consistently acting for the good, sin is a habit of choosing evil. It interrupts the loving relationship we should have with God.

The NDC lists the types of sin. Original sin "is the loss of the holiness and grace that Adam and Eve received from God" (n. 42D). It is the "fatal flaw" of all humans. Because of original sin, we are weakened and often inclined to sin. Even the holiest people commit venial sins, at times, because of temptation and the weakness of will that results from that first sin.

Personal sin comes in two kinds, mortal and venial. Mortal sin, as the name indicates, destroys our relationship with God. "Mortal sin is sin whose object is grave matter and which is committed with full knowledge and deliberate consent" (NDC, n. 42D). While not as serious as mortal sin, venial sin "diminishes or wounds the divine life in the soul and impairs the sinner's relationship with God" (NDC, n. 42D).

Again, those we teach need to understand that the best way to avoid sin is to try always to live virtuous lives. That should be a theme in all our moral catechesis.

It would help at this point in our discussion of morality to review in the NDC, n. 36B1: Catechesis for the Sacrament of Penance and Reconciliation; and n. 36B2: Catechesis for Children's First Reception of the Sacrament of Penance and Reconciliation. We can see now that Christ has provided, through the Church, a way for us to heal the broken relationship that led to sin. Through God's power, the sin can be forgiven and the relationship restored. A careful examination of conscience before receiving the sacrament provides an honest look at oneself and one's relationship with God through Jesus Christ.

The Human Community

An important area of moral theology is that of social justice. Down through history, people have exploited, enslaved, persecuted, or visited other ills on individuals or groups. Over the last century or so, there has been an increasing acknowledgment that the Church has a role to play in social justice. Pope Leo XIII's encyclical *On Capital and Labor*, 1891, emphasized our human destiny as social beings, and society's responsibility to support all people in their quest for life fulfillment. At the same time, each individual has a responsibility to support social structures that support life and human dignity and to correct those that do not.

The United States Conference of Catholic Bishops has highlighted seven themes of Catholic social teaching: (1) the life and dignity of the human person; (2) the call to family, community, and participation; (3) the rights and responsibilities of individuals and society; (4) the option for the poor and vulnerable; (5) the dignity of work and the rights of workers; (6) solidarity; and (7) care for God's creation. These themes and their meaning also need to become part of adult faith formation programs so that young people will not learn them in a vacuum and not see them applied by adults.

Finally, there is also social sin. Simply put, social sin is collective and is contributed to by the actions of many. Social sin is any condition in society that does not resemble the kingdom of God. Social sins include poverty, racism, sexism, economic injustice, environmental destruction, and the like. Part of an effective moral catechesis is helping those we teach understand how we all contribute to social sin and how we can work together to overcome it.

Conclusion

There are many riches in chapter six of the NDC. Take time to compare its suggestions with the topics covered in your catechetical textbook and supplements. Give special emphasis to those topics, and stress that a moral and virtuous life is how we show our love for God, who sent his Son, Jesus, to show us the way to our future life in God.

Your Thoughts

1 "In a secularist society there is a grave danger that people will live as if God did not exist" (NDC, 41B). This could be defined as an eclipse of God in culture. Is this my reality?

_____

_____

2 What techniques can I apply in my life and catechetical ministry to develop appropriate moral behavior? (Be specific.)

_____

_____

Try This

Using magazine pictures and newspaper headlines, create two collages, one that reflects elements of a culture of death and one that reflects elements of a culture of life. Discuss the challenges and opportunities we face in light of these two cultures. Write a prayer or compose a contemporary set of beatitudes that reflects a Christian moral response to your discovery.

PRAYING *with* CHRIST

LEISA ANSLINGER

As the disciples grew closer to Jesus, it seemed only natural that their relationship led them to say, "Lord, teach us to pray" (Luke 11:1b). They had seen Jesus withdraw to pray to his Father, and they surely recognized in Jesus the power of a person in deep communion with God. Drawn by their encounter with Christ, they sought to enter more deeply into the mystery of this relationship.

"Prayer is the basis and expression of the vital and personal relationship of a human person with the living and true God: 'God tirelessly calls each person to that mysterious encounter known as prayer'" (*National Directory for Catechesis*, n. 34). That "mysterious encounter" is essential to our lives as people of faith, and yet, it often eludes us. It is no wonder, then, that throughout the centuries we have said, "Lord, teach us to pray." The NDC guides us as we learn to pray and to teach others to hear God's tireless call to that mysterious encounter.

Catechesis Teaches Us to Pray with Christ

Born in the waters of baptism, we are immersed into Christ's life, death, and resurrection. This immersion leads us to pray with Christ as members of Christ's body, united with Christ and filled with the Spirit of

God. While in our humanity we may still be tempted to establish life independent of God's will, grace will always beckon us toward holiness.

As we mature as Christ's people, we learn to surrender the call of our selfish concerns and to seek union with God as our greatest desire. Jesus becomes for us our salvation and model for living: "Conversion to Christ and communion with him lead the faithful to adopt his disposition of prayer and reflection. Jesus' entire life, death, and Resurrection were an offering to his Father" (NDC, n. 20, 4).

Prayer feeds this lifetime of conversion by keeping us pointed heavenward as we offer thanksgiving, ask God's help, and seek forgiveness. We learn to join our suffering with Christ; our daily experiences become rich and meaningful in light of Christ's death and resurrection. United with Christ in prayer, our entire life becomes an offering to our Father.

Catechesis for All Ages

As we plan catechesis for people of all ages, we should consider the fullness of life in Christ. How do we invite people to embrace lifelong conversion? How do we provide catechetical opportunities for every age and stage of life? Often, it seems we overlook the real desire people have for God, and God for them (see NDC, n. 34).

> Catechesis leads individuals to fuller participation in the prayer of the community and...deepens our relationship with Christ.

When we really listen to people, we find that there are many ways of providing catechesis to meet the needs of people in a variety of stages in life. We can use short catechetical pieces in the parish bulletin, retreats and days of reflection, courses on sacred Scripture, prayer and catechetical sessions during the day and in the evening, links on our parish website, and book discussion groups. The possibilities are only limited by our imagination and the willingness to step out in faith.

Prayer to Catechesis to Prayer, Leading to Discipleship

There is a wonderful interrelationship between catechesis and prayer, especially the celebration of the liturgy. Catechesis leads individuals to fuller participation in the prayer of the community and as persons; prayer deepens our relationship with Christ, nurturing us and leading us to seek understanding (see NDC, n. 33).

Both prayer and catechesis form us as God's people, urging us to emulate Jesus' attention to the poor, blind, and lonely (in whatever form they manifest themselves), and to strive toward peace. We become more capable of living as Christian people as we are more conformed to Christ through catechesis and prayer.

Catechesis not only helps us better understand why we do what we do when we pray together but also leads us to reflect deeply on our lives in Christ. This, then, enables us to be fully present and ready to be formed by our communal celebration.

Think of the way the celebration of the sacred Triduum changes you over time and of the way your life changes from one Triduum to the next. The depth of the experience of Triduum is dependent upon many factors:

- How well have you marked your lenten journey leading up to Holy Thursday?

- Is the liturgy celebrated in a way that allows the ritual to speak of Christ's presence?

- Have you actively served others in a particular way?

- What has taken place in your life that you bring to the liturgy?

- Has someone you love been ill or did a special person in your life die this year?

- Have you known injustice?

- How have you changed as a result?

- From what have you asked for deliverance, and for what have you asked for forgiveness?

- In what ways do you as a catechetical leader or catechist invite others to plumb the depths of Christ's life and their lived experience, making such life-changing connections?

Catechesis through intergenerational gatherings, through a seasonal speaker series, in printed materials distributed on Sunday, and through discussions in small faith-sharing groups all help deepen the ways in which we live the feasts and seasons.

The rhythm of the liturgical year becomes our rhythm, with our personal prayer flowing from the Sunday celebration of the Eucharist. We may begin to pray the Divine Office or attend Evening Prayer at our parish. Or we may have a seasonal prayer space in our home that includes liturgical colors and a crucifix.

Seasonal catechesis helps us connect our experience of the liturgy with the rest of our lives in ways that often seem small and insignificant. Over time, however, the impact can be great, as we learn to recognize the ways in which "the liturgical year exerts 'a special sacramental power and influence which strengthens Christian life'" (NDC, n. 37A).

The Context of Catechesis Is Prayer

Strengthened as Christian people, we begin to seek ways to bring Christ's love to others through service—including the ministry of catechesis. As catechists, we recognize the value of prayer in our own lives, and therefore seek to share the riches of a vibrant prayer life with others.

While we might be tempted to relegate prayer as the topic of a few lessons with students each year, the NDC directs us differently: "Prayer should be the ordinary environment for all catechesis so that the knowledge and practice of the Christian life may be understood and celebrated in its proper context" (n. 20, 4).

Our lives as Christians flow from the Sunday liturgy. We are formed through catechesis and prayer that is inspired and gains its strength from the liturgy and the sacramental life of the Church. In this way, prayer also becomes the "ordinary environment" for catechesis. Prayer is not simply a topic to be covered once or twice a year with students. Instead, prayer is the air we breathe, the foundation of all our actions, the way in which we discern what to say, how to say it, when to remain silent, and when to speak.

> Prayer is the air we breathe, the foundation of all our actions, the way in which we discern what to say, how to say it, when to remain silent, and when to speak.

We will learn to catechize as Jesus did, becoming rooted in prayer ourselves, so that our entire lives become a prayer to our Father. Christ's way of teaching is our first and best example: "Christ's methodology was multi-dimensional. It included his words, his signs, and the wonders he worked...'The whole of Christ's life was a continual teaching: his silences, his miracles, his gestures, his prayer, his love for people, his special affection for the little and the poor, his acceptance of the total sacrifice on the Cross for the redemption of the world, and his Resurrection are the actualization of his word and the fulfillment of revelation'" (NDC, n. 28, 2).

Catechesis in which prayer is the "ordinary environment" has as its goal the formation of Christian people of all ages to live as disciples of Christ. It will build upon the rituals and symbols of our communal prayer and the images and colors of the liturgical seasons. It will be rooted in the knowledge that we encounter Christ through word and sacrament, as we gather together, and in the silence of our hearts. We will find that, rather than opening our time together with a prayer, prayer will become the fabric within which threads of teaching, sharing, questioning, dialoguing, serving, and proclaiming will be woven. Catechesis of this sort truly echoes God's word.

Teaching One Another to Pray with Christ

The message of Christ is that God seeks us out; God does not leave us to our own devices, tending to wander and stray. God's initiative comes first. Our response, prompted by the Holy Spirit, grows in time, as we recognize God's presence in time (see NDC, nos. 34 and 37). Prayer is a "mysterious encounter" with the One who tirelessly calls us, loving us beyond what we can conceive. Saying this and living it are often very different things, however. Too often we fall back on rote prayers that have little connection to the reality of our life, or we fail to allow prayers we have known since childhood to speak with the strength and power that is possible.

For many of us, prayer becomes a series of rushed moments of "talking at" God, rather than allowing it to be a dialogue in which the Holy Spirit "not only reveals the identity of the Triune God to human persons, but also reveals the identity of human persons to themselves" (NDC, n. 34).

Prayer that is open to God's working in us and with us is real. Real prayer gives voice to our deepest longings, our fiercest worries, our greatest fears, and our most ardent desires. Real prayer shapes us as one who is in Christ and, through Christ, is able to bring the whole of our being to God for consolation, strengthening, challenge, mercy, forgiveness, and love.

As communal people, we share prayer with one another in many ways. Some of us have within our family or ethnic group devotional prayers that are important to us. Such devotions may bring depth to the prayer of the community.

We pass on to our children and those who are catechumens and candidates other treasured prayers of our tradition, such as the Our Father, the Hail Mary, and the Rosary. The Liturgy of the Hours, and with it the Psalms, provides the framework for a lifetime of prayer, as we join our prayers with other Christians so that the Church prays always.

We teach one another to pray "by heart." The NDC reminds us of the importance of learning common prayers, factual information, formulas, and practices from memory. I would suggest that we also learn to pray "by heart," allowing our heart to reach out to the heart of all love. It is prayer "by heart" that remembers Christ's undying love. It is through prayer "by heart" that we recognize Christ's paschal mystery in our own lives, and in which we are transformed.

Prayer of this sort "is God's gift to the 'humble and contrite heart.' It expresses the covenant relationship that binds God to the person and the person to God. The connection is Christ…Personal prayer expresses communion with the life of the Blessed Trinity. The Holy Spirit inspires hearts to pray, removes obstacles to living life in Christ, and leads humanity into communion with the Father and the Son" (NDC, n. 34).

Conclusion

As disciples who are growing in relationship with Christ, it is natural and good for us to say, "Lord, teach us to pray." In Christ, we help one another learn the ways of prayer; we teach one another to pray in Christ. Through the power of the Holy Spirit, we find the grace to respond to God's tireless call to the "mysterious encounter known as prayer," in a "free self-surrender to the incomprehensible mystery of God" (NDC, n. 34). In this way, we will raise our hearts to God through Christ, so that our very lives will be a living prayer of love.

Your Thoughts

1 How has my encounter with God deepened or been challenged within the past two years?

_____

_____

2 How am I nurturing a vibrant life of prayer—communion with God—in and among my students? What are the challenges and opportunities I face?

_____

_____

Try This

Practice an hourly centering prayer. Sit quietly for a few moments. Let go of all distractions. Slowly repeat the classic Jesus Prayer, "Lord Jesus Christ, Son of God, have mercy on me, a sinner"; or pray, "Jesus, have mercy. Jesus, have mercy"; or "Jesus. Jesus. Jesus." This ancient prayer form has been the source of deep spiritual energy and life among many saints and ordinary people throughout history.

The LIFE *and* MISSION *of the* CHURCH

MARTIN ARSENAULT

A t its heart, catechesis is an apprenticeship in the life of a disciple. It is an apprenticeship that takes place in community. The community mentors and shapes the disciple, and the disciple is prepared through catechesis to enter more fully into the life of the community. The disciple is called to an ongoing process of more active participation that includes building up the community itself.

This process leads to a deepening relationship with Jesus Christ and a stronger bond with the members of the community of faith. It leads to an empowering of the imagination and moves the disciple to become someone who is thinking, acting, and living as a disciple.

Life of Communion

As Christian disciples, we are formed by our participation in the life of the parish community. The life of the community "catechizes" us. As the *National Directory for Catechesis* (NDC) notes, the whole community has responsibility for the mission of catechesis, and this mission is carried out in the midst of community. This mission is the mission of forming and sustaining mature adult disciples (see NDC, n. 53).

As the community prays, celebrates, shares belief, witnesses, serves, and acts for justice, it forms us. The Sunday celebration of the Eucharist forms us; the parish socials form us; the prayer groups and the charitable activities form us. Participation in the various ministries of the parish forms us. The intersection of our daily lives with the activities, hopes, dreams, joys, and sorrows of the members of the parish form us.

The community incorporates us into the life of communion; we become members of the community of disciples of the Lord. By living in community we live *into* community and become more united with the members of our parish. We learn the language of the faith in community just as we learn to speak in our households and in our neighborhoods. We are apprenticed in the faith through the rhythms, seasons, values, and symbols of the community. We are accepted into the community, and our story becomes incorporated into the story of the community.

> The catechist helps the disciple "fit in" to the life of discipleship and respond more completely to the baptismal call to conversion, witness, and community.

Within the life of the community and its mission of catechesis, there are moments and opportunities for more "formal" catechesis. Through this formal catechesis we initiate, form, and nurture members of the parish to live as disciples in community. We mentor these disciples more specifically and prepare them to live in and participate actively in the mission of the community in ever deeper ways. In these moments these disciples are mentored by one who is called and formed to be a catechist. The catechist helps the disciple "fit in" to the life of discipleship and respond more completely to the baptismal call to conversion, witness, and community.

Christian Community: Gift and Task

The Christian community has a twofold dimension. The first dimension is that community is a gift from God. As gift, the Christian community flows forth from the heart of the risen Lord. The Holy Spirit is sent by the risen Christ to bind his disciples together, and that same Spirit animates the community of disciples to continue his work, to be the sign of his presence in the world.

This gift is based on the call of Christ to form a community, a call answered by the very first disciples. It is based on the coming of the Spirit at Pentecost. It is a gift based on the promise of Christ that "where two or three are gathered together in my name, there am I in the midst of them" (Matthew 18:20).

The second dimension is that community is also a goal or task to be realized. The grace of God and the work of all the members of the community of disciples come together to accomplish this task. As task, the work of building community is a response to the gift given by Christ. It is a response to the prompting of the Holy Spirit to move the disciples of the Lord into unity with one another and into an ever deepening love for one another. As such, it is a response to Christ's command that we love one another. It is through this love that we gain our identity as disciples, for everyone knows that we are the Lord's disciples because of our love for one another (see John 13:34–35).

Catechesis Prepares the Christian to Live in Community

Catechesis prepares us to respond to the two-fold dimension of community. Catechesis opens up for us the fullness of the gift of community. We "learn" about the Lord's great love for us and about the presence of the Holy Spirit in our midst. We are introduced to this teaching, and we have that teaching connected to our daily life, our human experience, our life of prayer, our call to form ourselves into mature moral agents, and our life of service and witness (see NDC, n. 20).

Catechesis prepares us to take up the task of building up the community of disciples. We "learn" the values and attitudes we must adopt to live in harmony and in an animated way with our brother and sister disciples. We learn to overcome the obstacles to true Christian love, and we are shown the virtues that support and nurture true Christian community. We learn Christ's teaching about community life, which calls us to simplicity, humility, solidarity with and concern for the poor, common prayer, mutual forgiveness, and fraternal love (see NDC, n. 20, 5).

Catechesis prepares us to be active and conscious members of the community in a variety of ways. In all facets of catechesis, we learn together how to live as mature, committed disciples of the Lord. We learn to love one another as Christ has loved us in the concrete reality of parish life. We support and challenge one another, and serve as examples to one another regarding the teachings of Christ on community life.

Catechesis prepares us to live in community by putting us into communion with Christ—with his actions, words, and values. Catechesis encourages us to live a life patterned on Christ, to live virtuously, simply, and with the humility and faith of a little child.

Catechesis puts us in touch with the meanings and realities of the kingdom of God, which in turn moves us to concern and action on behalf of the poor and marginalized. As we pray for, support, and act on behalf of the poor and marginalized, we grow more fully into the community of disciples the Lord intends us to be. We gradually and surely live as more mature Christian disciples. As this process continues, we become more aware of the many ways in which we are called to live the Christian life and the many ways we are united as a community of believers. We grow in our awareness of our connectedness to all Christian communities, Catholic and non-Catholic, and we grow in our respect for the religious beliefs of all people of good will.

Active Participation in the Life of the Church

All catechesis prepares us to participate actively in the life of the Church. Catechesis is an ecclesial act that stems from the community and directs all of its efforts back toward the life of the community. Catechesis teaches us that life in community is a life for others; a life for the sake of the kingdom of God; a life of peacemaking, reconciliation, justice, and sanctifying the daily lives of all the members. We are called into immersion into one another's lives. We are called to profess and hold certain beliefs in common: to pray, break bread, serve, and know and meet the needs of the poor and marginalized—together.

Catechesis prepares the disciple to participate actively in the life of the parish community. We "learn" that our participation includes the weekly celebration of the Sunday Eucharistic liturgy, which is the source and main expression of our unity in the Lord. We learn that we are to celebrate the sacraments for the sake of our own faith journey and the faith life of the community.

In catechesis we are encouraged to support the parish by giving of our time, God-given gifts, and financial resources. We are to strengthen the relationships among the members of the community so that we may serve together in harmony and unity. We are to gather for festive events to celebrate our common life and the story of our unique community.

Active Participation in the Mission of the Church

Every community of disciples participates in the mission of Christ. Every parish is an instance of the people of God gathering together to announce and help bring about the kingdom of God. As we work on behalf of the kingdom of God, we carry on the mission of Christ in the community and the world. We fulfill the mission entrusted to the Church.

Catechesis prepares us to participate in the many ministries that seek to fulfill the mission of Christ in the parish. Those ministries include: proclaiming the Good News, evangelizing, initiating into the community, celebrating the sacraments, ministering to the grieving, catechizing, serving the poor and marginalized, and reaching out in charity and justice.

Catechesis forms and prepares all disciples in the community who are called by their baptism to serve the mission by responding to the needs of the community. Catechesis also forms disciples for a particular ministry by providing the foundations and experiences needed to gain the competency to serve that part of the mission.

Catechists: Models and Examples of Catholic Community

Catechists are models of the Catholic Christian community. They make present to their learners the parish, the universal Church, and the dialogue with other religions. Catechists are "bridges" to the community for the learners they are forming in the faith. They are bridges for the community to the disciples. In a real sense, catechists are the point of unity, the embodiment of the unity to which the whole community is called. As this embodiment, catechists need to be strong models of committed community life.

Catechists—by nature of their commitment to serve—are signs of commitment to the community and the ministry of the community. Other members of the community should be able to look to the catechist for hints and patterns of how to live a life of active participation in the life and ministry of the parish community. The catechist's participation in the worship of the community should be visible, rich, informed, and full.

> Catechists—by nature of their commitment to serve— are signs of commitment to the community and the ministry of the community.

As models and examples, catechists need to be immersed in the life of the community at all levels without necessarily being involved directly in any other specific ministries. They need to know the many ministries that the parish supports for the advancement of the kingdom of God. For example, the catechist should be familiar with: the members of the baptismal preparation team, those who serve on the bereavement ministry team, the parish deacons, the liturgical ministers, the members of the social concerns team, etc. Immersion in the life of the community, however, goes beyond familiarity with the various members of particular ministries. The catechist should be in regular communication with these members to be aware of the people they are serving.

As a model of community commitment and involvement, catechists should cultivate a spirit of solidarity with those members of the community who are poor or alienated in any way. They should seek to live a life of simplicity for the sake of the gospel. They should strive to be examples of those who are free from the snare of consumerism and the acquiring of many possessions.

Catechists should be models of the love of neighbor Christ calls all the baptized to embrace (see John 13:34). They should cultivate the virtue of humility, especially in the exercising of the ministry of catechesis, being aware that they serve in this ministry on behalf of the community, through the Holy Spirit, to fulfill Christ's mission. They should be aware that it is an awesome privilege and gift to be called to journey with another in faith.

The Spiritual Life of the Catechist

As a catechist, take every opportunity to deepen your own relationship to the Lord—your own communion with Christ and with the members of your own faith community.

Look to the members of your parish community to find some people who are examples of simplicity, humility, solidarity, and communal love. Pray with them, engage them in conversation, and meditate on their words and deeds. This will allow you a direct connection to your faith community and open you to a deeper apprenticeship in the life of Christian discipleship.

Look to the liturgical seasons and how your community is celebrating them for themes or insights in the Scriptures, the prayers, and the symbols that will take you deeper into some aspect of community.

Your Thoughts

1 In the community of my parish, what has helped me appreciate my own "apprenticeship of Christian life"?

_____

_____

_____

2 How do I bring the stories and concerns of the local community into my catechetical ministry?

_____

_____

_____

Try This

Graph your personal stages of "apprenticeship of the Christian life." Indicate how ongoing faith formation is intentionally or consciously realized in your life. Name the challenges you still face.

CHRISTIANS *in* SOCIETY

LAVERNE E. BERTIN

Who we are and what we believe matters. It matters to the individual, to the family, to the local community, and ultimately, to the global society. Inhabitants of the twenty-first century are being summoned repeatedly to confront this underlying reality.

While this truth remains applicable to it all, it holds particular significance for catechists and their learners. This sixth task of catechesis acknowledges this reality as it challenges each of us to live according to what we believe. In many ways this task can be seen as an outcome of the five that precede it. All of the tasks are in some way oriented toward discipleship.

In this chapter we examine a three-step cyclical process from conversion to discipleship to serving the mission of the Church.

This diagram shows the cyclical process of Conversion, Discipleship, and Mission. The inner circles are the three theological virtues, which reflect the divine life, activity, and gifts of the Trinity, i.e., from hope we receive faith, out of faith we return charity, and in charity we offer hope to others.

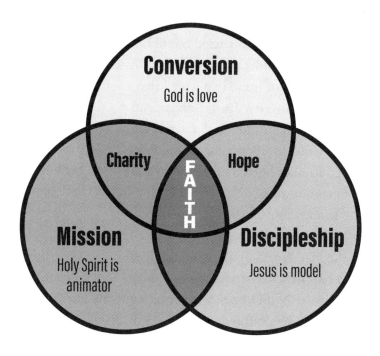

Sound catechesis understands conversion as a lifelong process; discipleship as a response to conversion; and missionary spirit as an outcome of mature discipleship (see *General Directory for Catechesis*, n. 46).

Catechesis Promotes a Missionary Spirit

Promoting a missionary spirit necessitates communicating a clear understanding of what the primary mission of the Church is. Pope Paul VI proclaimed this mission to be "bringing the Good News of the Gospel into all the strata of humanity, and through its influence transforming humanity from within and making it new" (see *Evangelization in the Modern World*, n. 18).

Jesus, the embodied Good News of God, is the primary model for developing a missionary spirit in the Church. He declared his mission in the world when he disclosed to his followers: "I must proclaim the good news of the kingdom of God, because for this purpose I have been sent" (see Mark 1:38; Luke 4:43). He proclaimed the Good News of the kingdom of God through his words and deeds and by the way in which he lived. In other words, Jesus acted out of his own convictions.

When catechists follow the example set by Jesus, they become who they are: harbingers of hope in a world that is often disheartened because of isolation, poverty, disease, abuse, and violence. Hope is the posture faith takes when it looks into the future. Being formed in faith impacts the future of both the individual and the Church community.

> Hope is the posture faith takes when it looks into the future.

Sitting somewhere in the classroom of a catechist at this moment might be the future leader of the Free World or a potential Hitler (who was a baptized Roman Catholic). There might be a future Nobel Prize winner or someone lost in chemically induced darkness. Undoubtedly there are seats in the class that remain empty because persons in that parish are absent—either by design, through neglect, or due to the lack of an invitation.

It matters to learners who their catechists are, what they believe, and whether or not they are present to them. Catechists should never envision themselves as "just parish volunteers." Catechists can be seen as those who serve Christ in a specific place and at a particular time to the best of their ability and the extent of their training and support. Today, every catechist has been entrusted with the sacred mission begun by Jesus. By virtue of this mission, she or he becomes a front-line evangelizer.

Whoa...Evangelization? Not Me!

Many Catholics have an unenthusiastic response when they hear the word *evangelization*. Often this is caused by one of three viewpoints.

FIRST, the way in which a word is interpreted today is prejudiced by the way it has been used in the past. Hearing the word *evangelization* can conjure up images of in-your-face encounters with people going door to door or holding forth on radio or on TV.

A contemporary Catholic understanding of evangelization has furthering the reign of God as its primary goal. The process of evangelization is animated by the Holy Spirit and carried out by both the community and its individuals.

In this way of thinking, conversion is not seen as a one-time event, and there is no time constraint put on the process. Instead, conversion is regarded as a free and informed choice made in response to God's initiative and the prompting of the Holy Spirit throughout life. It continues until the very last breath one takes on earth (see NDC, n. 17B).

SECOND, many see faith as a private matter and not something to be shared with others. It is true that mature conversion is the acceptance of a personal relationship with Christ, and it is a personal decision to become a disciple. Nevertheless, once a person chooses to become a disciple, he or she becomes united with the larger community of disciples and assumes the faith of the Church (see NDC, n. 17B).

For Catholics, faith is not just a matter of self-edification or personal salvation. It is a lived response to the loving God who created us all. We are called to communion with Christ and with one another. In the Judeo-Christian tradition, we are all simultaneously sacred and social beings. We are sacred because we are made in the image of God (see Genesis 1:26–27), and social because we literally cannot live except in relationship to God and others (see Genesis 2:18).

THIRD, an unenthusiastic response to the concept of evangelization may stem from someone who does not know *how* to share his or her faith and is, therefore, uncomfortable at the prospect of being asked to do so.

Through the Holy Spirit, each of us has been given three basic missionary tools: the power to witness from our own experience; the desire to form community; and the capacity to proclaim the gospel in accordance with our own unique gifts and roles in life (see *Catechism of the Catholic Church*, nos. 737–741).

Catechesis That Prepares the Faithful...

If we are to "prepare Christians to be present in society" we must first help them to envision discipleship as something to be lived into, rather than a once-in-a-lifetime commitment. And we must engage them in meaningful conversations about life and faith. This means honestly asking ourselves where and how we are providing practical opportunities for sincere and sustained dialogue among Christians today.

Age-appropriate dialogue and reflection on teachings or content are two necessary elements in good faith formation. Developing these skills early in life can help learners better integrate faith and life and avoid creating a false dichotomy between the two.

God's word doesn't change, but our ability to hear it and live it does. Questions should be seen as opportunities for children, adolescents, and adults to discover more about their faith and what God is calling them to be or do. It has been said that the most meaningful theological question is, "So what?" That is to say, what does this passage from Scripture, this teaching, this ritual, or this tradition have to do with my life, my family, my work, my friends? Soul-searching questions provide opportunities to enter into the mysteries of our faith.

...To Be Present as Christians in Society

The sixth task of catechesis names the world as the place and means for the lay faithful to fulfill their vocations. It is within this world that we walk, work, and worship with others (see *Pastoral Constitution on the Church in the Modern World*, n. 2).

When Jesus walked this earth with others, he engaged them in conversation about God and their faith. In response to a question, he gave us his Greatest Commandment; "The first is this: 'Hear, O Israel! The Lord our God is Lord alone! You shall love the Lord your God with all your heart, with all your soul, with all your mind, and with all your strength.'

The second is this: 'You shall love your neighbor as yourself. There is no other commandment greater than these'" (Mark 12:29–31; also see Matthew 22:37–40; Luke 10:25–28).

While the love of neighbor is a path that leads us to the encounter with God, closing our eyes to our neighbor can also blind us to God. When catechists constantly promote an awareness of the "other," they too bring their learners and themselves closer to the kingdom of God.

The first human question asked in the Bible is "Am I my brother's keeper?" (Genesis 4:9). Thousands of years later, human beings still pose that question, and the way in which we answer this question governs the choices we make and the actions we take. Without a doubt, our own answer to this question determines the way we live our lives.

> "Demonstrate your faith to me without works and I will demonstrate my faith to you from my works."
>
> **JAMES 2:18**

Listen to what James asserts in this powerful passage: "What good is it, my brothers, if someone says he has faith but does not have works? Can that faith save him? If a brother or sister has nothing to wear and has no food for the day, and one of you says to them, 'Go in peace, keep warm, and eat well' but you do not give them the necessities of the body, what good is it? So also faith of itself, if it does not have works, is dead. Indeed someone might say, 'You have faith and I have works.' Demonstrate your faith to me without works and I will demonstrate my faith to you from my works" (James 2:14–18).

Through the Works of Mercy, the Church has provided us a wonderful teaching that builds on this scriptural insight (see *Catechism of the Catholic Church*, n. 2447). The Corporal Works of Mercy address the physical needs of our brothers and sisters, such as the ones of which James speaks. We exhibit our concern for the well-being of our brothers and sisters when we feed the hungry, give drink to the thirsty, clothe the naked, shelter the homeless, comfort the imprisoned, visit the sick, and bury the dead.

The Spiritual Works of Mercy benefit others and serve to fulfill the mission of the Church. We demonstrate our love for our brothers and sisters by admonishing sinners (without judging), instructing the uninformed, counseling the doubtful, comforting the sorrowful, being patient with those who err, forgiving offenses against us, and praying for the living and the dead. At some point during our lifetimes, all of us will be in need of these good works. It is through God's mercy that someone will be there for us.

Who Are Our Brothers and Sisters?

The previously mentioned narrative of Jesus giving the Greatest Commandment is found in all three of the synoptic gospels. But it is the Gospel of Luke that challenges us to go a bit further. The young man who questions Jesus continues the conversation by asking one more question: "And who is my neighbor?" (Luke 10:29).

As we hear Jesus recount the familiar parable of the good Samaritan, we can envision this traveler as a person acting out of his own beliefs. His compassion dictates that he must stop and show mercy to the victim of a robbery. It doesn't matter to him that the victim belongs to a group of people who, for ethnic and religious reasons, is in bitter opposition with his own community. Jesus helps the young inquirer to understand that the Samaritan man was right in recognizing the "other" as his neighbor. Then Jesus tells him, "Go and do likewise" (Luke 10:37).

Actions we identify as works of mercy are performed daily by decent, dedicated people out of their genuine concern for others, their professional training, or their faith beliefs. Catechists can help their learners celebrate all that is right in the world by recognizing the righteousness of others, including those who may witness to a faith other than our own. They can also lead others to imagine what the world would be like if there were mutual understanding and genuine peace among religions today.

As members of God's global community, we are called to give consideration to the things that unite us and to what we the people have in common. The Church teaches that other religions deserve our esteem because they represent the living expression of the spirituality of vast groups of people. These are people who have spent thousands of years praying, asking profound human questions, and searching for God—often with great sincerity and virtuous hearts. The major religions are Muslim, Hindu, Buddhist, and Christian. (And there are more than 9,000 Christian denominations worldwide.) The Catholic Church does not reject anything that is true and holy in any of these religions and indeed encourages prudent and open dialogue with others.

Ecumenism: To Inhabit the World Together

We believe that God established one true Church. And yet, scandalously, we are not truly "one" with our Christian brothers and sisters today. Before Jesus was arrested, he prayed fervently for his disciples and for those who would follow their witness to him. He pleaded that his disciples would all become one as he was with the Father. His concern was that if *they* were not united, the world might not believe in *him* (see John 17:11).

Much progress has been made in ecumenical dialogue among Christian churches since the groundbreaking documents of Vatican II. Nevertheless, there is an immediate need to share in Jesus' concern about our ability to witness to him by doing more locally and globally to promote unity.

The *Decree on Ecumenism* (n. 4) lists five ways for individuals and groups to promote unity:

1] Commit to learning more truth about our faith and that of others in order to overcome false perceptions and prejudices;

2] Join together in dialogue;

3] Cooperate with one another and work together to address the needs of the marginalized in our society;

4] Join one another in prayer;

5] Carefully examine our own beliefs to discern if they are attuned to the will of Christ.

While we believe that the Catholic Church provides the fullness of the means of salvation, we recognize that salvation is not limited to Catholics—or to Christians (see *On Evangelization in the Modern World*, n. 53). We believe that the mercy of God and "salvation in Jesus Christ is intended for all people despite their social, cultural, racial, ethnic, or economic differences" (NDC, n. 52). In charity and hope for one another, we continue to seek understanding and peace. Everyone may not belong to this Church, but all are included in the reach of its embrace (see *Dogmatic Constitution on the Church*, n. 9).

As far as we know, there were no eyewitnesses to the resurrection. Accepting this mystery is a matter of faith, hope, and trust. Why then, have millions of people come to believe what their eyes have not seen?

For thousands of years, people have encountered those who have borne witness to the paschal mystery. Their lives have been visibly transformed by an encounter with the living Christ. It is through the words, deeds, and actions of these ordinary people that countless others have come to know Christ.

Ordained and lay people have been entrusted by God, by virtue of their baptism, to live and work in this world so that the divine message of salvation may be known and accepted by all. It is *only* through our beliefs and actions that others can hear the gospel and come to know Christ (see *Catechism of the Catholic Church*, n. 900).

Every one of us has a circle of influence in life: in our homes, at work, in school, and wherever we may be. Whether we recognize it or not, we are constantly influencing others in a positive or a negative way. Through the gifts of courage and joy, we can begin asking of ourselves: "What am I doing to build the kingdom of God today?" The smallest acts of kindness, mercy, or faith sharing can have a ripple effect beyond our imagination. The key is doing something for God and others in an intentional and ongoing manner. Recall the words of St. Mother Teresa:

"What I can do, you cannot. What you can do, I cannot. But together, we can do something beautiful for God."

Conclusion

Catechists can help others remember that God is the reason for all creation and grants us not only our existence but also the dignity of acting on our own and being causes and principles for one another as we cooperate in God's plan of salvation (see CCC, n. 306).

In light of this, all of us need to summon the strength to critically examine who we are and what we believe. It is up to each of us to bring the gospel message out into the world we live in. If we believe what we teach and teach it like we believe it, seeds of hope will be planted throughout the world, and others can grow to become who they are called to be: people of God manifesting a divine love of the other.

Your Thoughts

1 How do I see my "missionary activity" within the Church? How do I inspire my students to understand their call to discipleship as a "missionary activity"? (Be specific.)

_____

_____

_____

2 What does the following statement mean to me? "God's word doesn't change but our ability to hear it and live it does."

_____

_____

_____

Try This

Reflect on the Spiritual and Corporal Works of Mercy. Use pictures or stories that reflect the realization of these works in our world today; or prepare a PowerPoint presentation on these to share with your students.

ABOUT THE CONTRIBUTORS

General Editor

Sr. Angela Ann Zukowski, MHSH, D.Min, is the Director of the Institute for Pastoral Initiatives (1978-present) and Professor in the Department of Religious Studies of the University of Dayton. She is a member of the Mission Helpers of the Sacred Heart (Towson, MD), and was the Executive Editor for the University of Dayton *Catechist Formation Series* published by CATECHIST magazine.

Chapter 1

Sue Grenough, Ed.D. MRE, has worked in the field of catechesis as an elementary parish catechist, a high school religion teacher, a director of religious education, and a diocesan director of catechesis. She was instrumental in composing the religion curriculum guidelines for the state of Kentucky. She is currently an adjunct professor at Spalding University in Louisville, KY.

Chapter 2

Rose L. Bennett is the former coordinator for evangelization, adult catechesis, and adult initiation for the Archdiocese of Baltimore. As a parish DRE for more than 20 years, she is experienced in both catechumenal and catechetical ministry. She is the author of *Evangelization in the Parish Catechetical Program*, published by NCCL.

Chapter 3

Joyce Ann Zimmerman, CPPS, is the director of the Institute for Liturgical Ministry in Dayton, Ohio, and is an adjunct professor of liturgy, liturgical

consultant, and frequent facilitator of workshops. She is a consultant to the Committee on Divine Worship and has published numerous scholarly and pastoral liturgical works. She holds civil and pontifical doctorates of theology.

Chapter 4

Patrick R. Guentert is a retired Diocesan Director of Religious Education living in Niles, MI. He has degrees in theology and religious education and has thirty-five years' experience in religious education as a parish and diocesan director of religious education.

Chapter 5

Leisa Anslinger, MA, is Director of Catholic Life and Faith in Loveland, OH, a resource center for pastoral leaders in dioceses and parishes. She is the former Pastoral Associate for Evangelization, Catechesis and Stewardship at Immaculate Conception of Mary Parish in Cincinnati and is a frequent workshop presenter and contributor to catechetical publications.

Chapter 6

Martin J. Arsenault is a catechetical professional and former Director of the Office of Catechesis in Trenton, NJ, and lives in Hightstown, NJ.

Chapter 7

LaVerne E. Bertin, MRE, is Associate Director of Religious Education for the Diocese of Worcester, MA. She directs the certification of catechists as well as the Adult Education and Faith Formation programs.

RECOMMENDED RESOURCES

The following are available from the United States Conference of Catholic Bishops or your local Catholic bookstore

National Directory for Catechesis. Washington, DC: United States Conference of Catholic Bishops, 2005

General Directory for Catechesis. Washington, DC. Congregation for the Clergy. United States Conference of Catholic Bishops, 1997

Our Hearts Were Burning Within Us. United States Conference of Catholic Bishops, Washington, DC. 1999

New American Bible, Revised Edition (NABRE), 2011 (also available online at www.usccb.org/bible)

The following are available at your local Catholic bookstore or online at www.vatican.va.

On Catechesis in Our Time. Apostolic Exhortation of Pope John Paul II, 1979

Dogmatic Constitution on the Church. Pope Paul VI, 1964

On Evangelization in the Modern World. Pope Paul VI, 1975
Decree on Ecumenism, Pope Paul VI, 1964

The Gospel of Life, Pope John Paul II, 1995

On Capital and Labor, Pope Leo XIII, 1891

Catechism of the Catholic Church. Vatican City. Second Edition. 1997